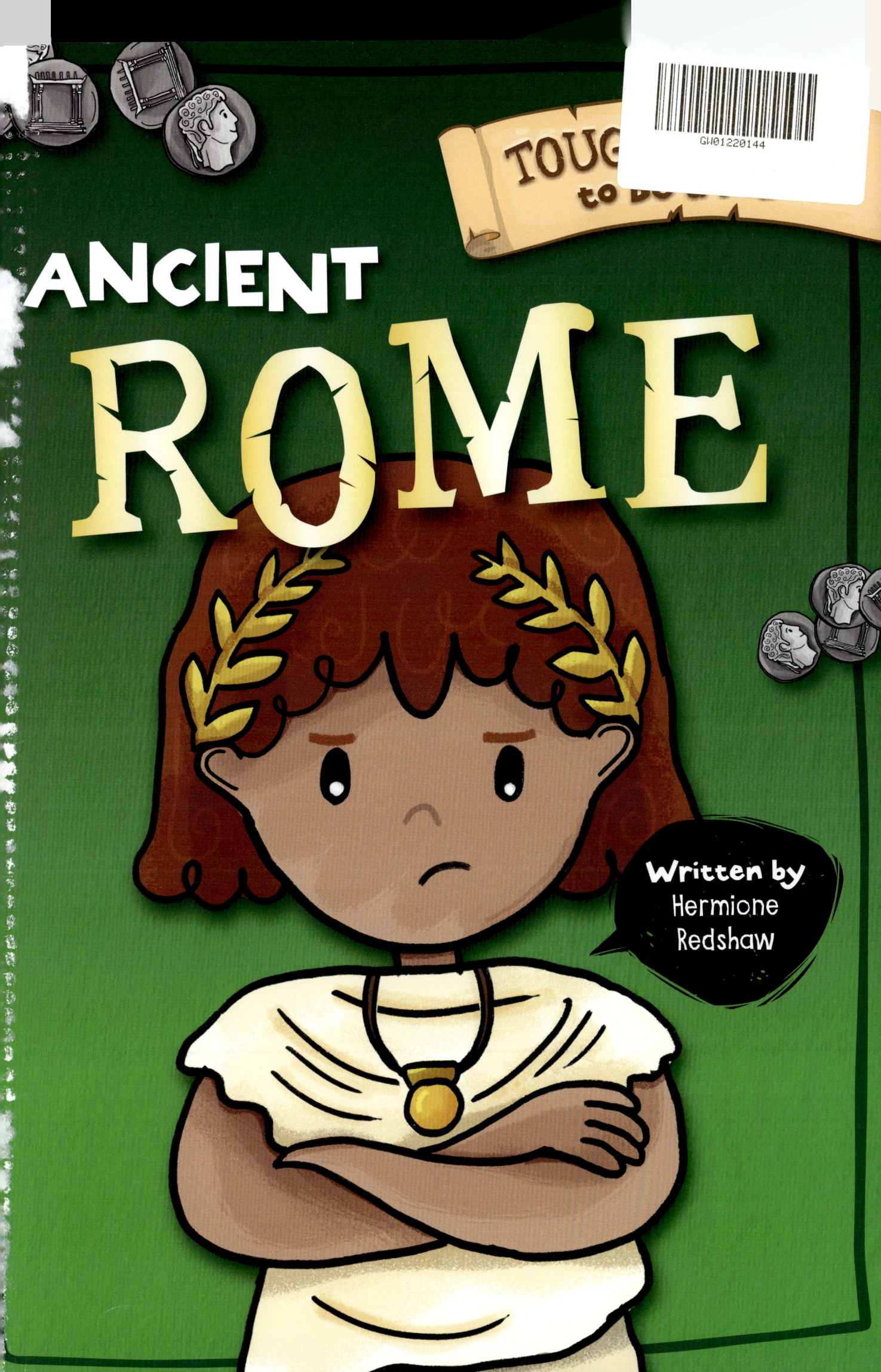

BookLife PUBLISHING

©2023
BookLife Publishing Ltd.
King's Lynn, Norfolk
PE30 4LS, UK

All rights reserved.
Printed in Poland.

A catalogue record for this book is available from the British Library.

ISBN: 978-1-80155-847-1

Written by:
Hermione Redshaw

Edited by:
Robin Twiddy

Designed and illustrated by:
Amy Li

All facts, statistics, web addresses and URLs in this book were verified as valid and accurate at time of writing. No responsibility for any changes to external websites or references can be accepted by either the author or publisher.

WEST SUSSEX SCHOOLS LIBRARY SERVICE	
10S749936	
Askews & Holts	25-Jul-2023
937	

CONTENTS

Page 4   Being a Kid
Page 6   Ancient Rome
Page 8   Surviving the Time
Page 10   Familia Faces
Page 12   Home Sweet Rome
Page 14   Snail Salad
Page 16   Singing and Sacrifices
Page 18   Tunic or not Tunic?
Page 20   Splinter the Teddy Bear
Page 22   Class by Candlelight
Page 26   Grown Up at What Age?
Page 30   That's Tough!
Page 31   Glossary
Page 32   Index

Words that look like this are explained in the glossary on page 31.

Being a KID

It's tough being a kid. School days are long, there are so many rules for crossing the street, and vegetables will never be as good as sweets, no matter how good parents say they are for you.

Now, imagine living in a time where school happens seven days a week, sewage flows down the middle of the street and vegetables might make up a whole meal. You have just imagined what it was like to live in ancient Rome.

NOT THE PEAS!

Do you think being a kid is tough today? Well, you had better prepare yourself for what you're about to read. Ancient Rome really was a tough time to be a kid.

If you're ready, let's travel back in time. You can see for yourself what life was really like for a child in ancient Rome.

Ancient ROME

Ancient Rome began with the building of the city of Rome, which started in 753 BC. The Romans had a large empire that ruled many parts of Europe for nearly 1,000 years. Rome's way of living was spread across Europe during this time.

Hello, Europe! You are now part of the Roman Empire! Want to see how we do things?

Some things we do or have today came from ancient Rome. The ancient Romans built roads with pavements. They were the first to bind their scrolls into books. They also added January and February to our calendar!

Now that January is in the calendar, I can finally celebrate my birthday.

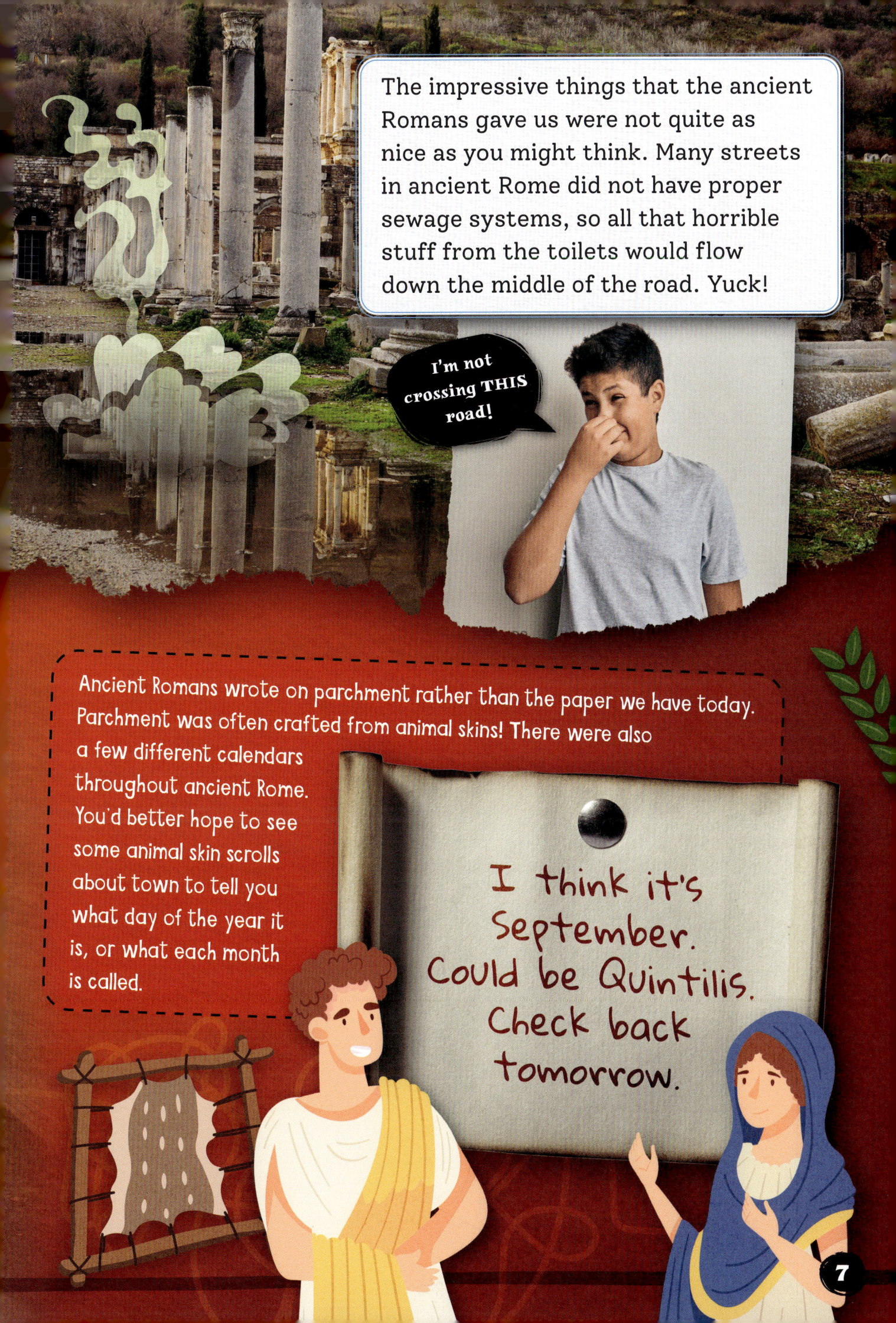

The impressive things that the ancient Romans gave us were not quite as nice as you might think. Many streets in ancient Rome did not have proper sewage systems, so all that horrible stuff from the toilets would flow down the middle of the road. Yuck!

I'm not crossing THIS road!

Ancient Romans wrote on parchment rather than the paper we have today. Parchment was often crafted from animal skins! There were also a few different calendars throughout ancient Rome. You'd better hope to see some animal skin scrolls about town to tell you what day of the year it is, or what each month is called.

I think it's September. Could be Quintilis. Check back tomorrow.

SURVIVING the Time

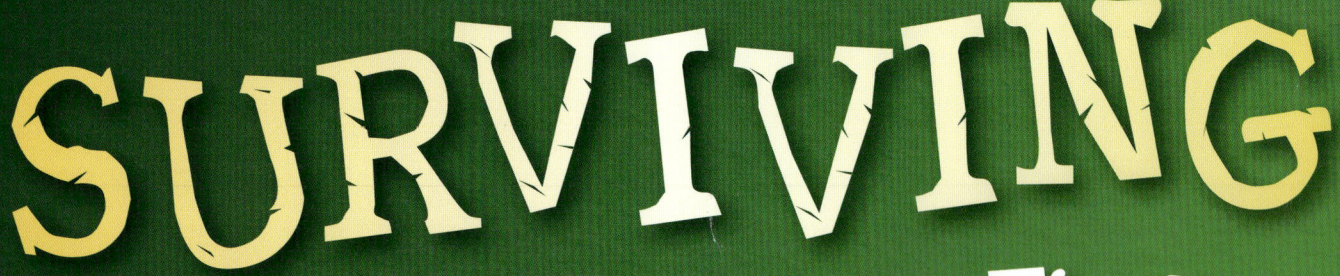

To get to all of the strange things that made being a kid in ancient Rome tough, first you needed to survive. That might sound easy. However, things we don't worry about now might have meant the end for you in ancient Rome.

What am I looking at?

If you're older than one year old, then congratulations! You have survived longer than around one in four Roman babies. However, your parents might not seem too thrilled around you for a while. Ancient Romans did not believe that babies were fully human.

What am I, some sort of alien?

If you survived for longer than 40 days, you might then become a person in your parents' eyes. That was the most difficult time to survive. Children would finally be seen as human once they could walk and talk.

Now that you are a person, son, let me teach you how to make pots.

The reason that some children did not survive often came down to healthcare. Doctors and medicine play a huge part in keeping people alive today. Ancient Roman doctors, on the other hand, relied on herbs and prayers to keep their patients alive.

Don't worry, sir. A few prayers and some vinegar will have you good as new.

FAMILIA Faces

The ancient Roman family was known as the 'familia'. Families were strong alliances where having lots of people in the familia was important. If anyone left home or went away from their family, they might still be seen as part of the familia.

Hey, you look familia...

Thanks for adopting me, Dad.

No problem, son. Now, go win that election!

If a Roman had no children to carry on their family name, they would adopt. Adoption brought families together. In one case, a man adopted someone older than him, Claudius, so that he could run for an election.

"Don't look at me."

The head of the household would be the oldest male. They were known as the paterfamilias, meaning father of the family. He would have power over everyone. If he wanted to, he could <u>disown</u> his children, sell them or much worse.

Don't mess with Dad!

Children had to do anything their parents told them to do. You never talked back to your older family members in ancient Rome. Doing so could get you thrown out of the house and never allowed back. Yikes!

HOME Sweet ROME

Romans with lots of money lived in a domus. This was a house built around a courtyard known as an atrium. Rich Roman houses had many rooms, including a room for a bath. Having your own bath was rare in ancient Rome!

Being rich didn't always mean you were living a life of luxury. Using the bathroom was a social thing in ancient Rome, so even rich homes may have had latrines. These are benches with holes in them that ancient Romans used as toilets.

I think I'll hold it!

Poor people lived in buildings called insulae. The buildings had lots of smaller houses over as many as nine floors, and no lift to get to the top. They only had one or two rooms for the whole family, so you might have to share a bedroom with your mum, dad, brothers, sisters and more!

So many steps!

Cooking was often done in a shared courtyard outside and wasn't always safe. Roman homes were often destroyed by fire. A big fire, called the Great Fire of Rome, destroyed a large amount of Rome. It took six days to put out!

Well, there goes another home.

SNAIL Salad

A WHAT salad?

Ancient Romans ate lots of vegetables. Believe it or not, cabbage was one of the most popular foods! Poor Romans had an even less exciting time. They often ate dried peas.

Mum, why do those kids get cabbage while we only have dried peas? They're SO lucky!

I've been walking for weeks to get these oranges!

Is there one fruit you love more than others? You might not get your favourite fruit from a quick visit to the shop in ancient Rome. Some fruits could be grown nearby. Others, such as oranges and cherries, came from faraway places. The journey to get them could be long...

Don't worry. It wasn't all fruit and vegetables for a meal in ancient Rome. Ancient Romans sometimes ate grains, such as bread, and meat. However, if you're expecting a beef burger, you might need to think again. Meat was a little bit different back then.

YUCK!

Meat came from animals such as hare, boar and... flamingo? It also included smaller animals such as mice and snails. Yuck! Those fruits and vegetables probably don't sound so bad now!

SINGING
and Sacrifices

Is my name Neptune or Poseidon? Even I don't know anymore!

The ancient Romans worshipped lots of gods and goddesses. They shared many beliefs with the ancient Greeks, such as stories about the gods creating the world. However, the ancient Romans had their own names for each god.

Children often took part in ceremonies and celebrations for the gods. They might be asked to sing in choirs. They might also help with sacrifices to the gods. One of those definitely sounds better than the other…

Two Roman children ready to sacrifice their first goat… or sing… one of the two.

Roman children had to worship the household gods. They even had to do chores for their gods. If you didn't do this, bad things might happen to you or your family.

Sweep the floor or your dinner will be mysteriously struck by lightning!

Vesta

Families would look after their own fires, known as hearths, even if they had people who could do it for them. This was to honour the goddess of the hearth and home, Vesta. Honouring Vesta might involve throwing something precious into the fire.

Well, I hope Vesta is happy, because I am not.

TUNIC
or not Tunic?

Do you ever wonder what you might wear for the day when you wake up in the morning? Well, children in ancient Rome did not have that problem. Unlike some of the adult Romans you might see in pictures, Roman children only had one thing to wear.

This is what all the kids are wearing... literally!

I HATE THIS!

Both boys and girls wore tunics. Boys wore their tunic down to their knees, while girls' tunics were longer and worn with a woollen belt tied around their waists. Rich children might even have had it worse for once. They wore togas.

You can forget about adding some colour to your ancient Roman wardrobe, too. Clothes were usually white. There were no bright colours, fancy patterns or logos across tunics. It all sounds very boring.

Children also wore a special charm called a bulla. It would be given to them when they were a few days old. The charm protected them from evil spirits, so you wouldn't want to lose yours!

Oh no! My one weakness!

SPLINTER the Teddy Bear

PLAY WITH ME!

There were no video games in ancient Rome. Children would play with dolls and animals made from wood, wax and clay. It must have been hard to snuggle up with a wooden bear at night!

Ancient Romans also used bones for some toys! Knucklebones was a popular game in ancient times, which was played using small bones from animals.

Last night's dinner gave me these new toys!

Awesome! Let's play!

20

The ancient Romans made lots of board games. Some of their games are similar to games played today, such as noughts and crosses, chess and checkers. You know, those games you might only play if you lost your tablet charger.

Tabula

I would kill for a good video game right about now!

Now, which one do I want to play with?

Most Roman toys were educational, meaning they helped kids to learn. Where's the fun in that? Fortunately, many Roman children found them entertaining. Then again, they didn't know about the toys we have today!

Class by CANDLELIGHT

Schools similar to the ones we know today existed in ancient Rome. However, they were only for boys. Actually, they were only for the richest of boys.

What do you mean I'm lucky? I don't want to go to school!

I have to go to school every day of the week!

School started before sunrise. That means you could be there really early in summer when days are longer! There was no <u>electricity</u>, either. Students had to use candles or oil lamps. They would work until late afternoon. This would be repeated seven days a week!

Where's the plus button?

Roman kids mostly learnt reading, writing and basic maths. That might not sound so bad, except your calculator might look a little different and your books could be written in either Latin or Greek! Ancient Romans also had to learn how to speak in front of crowds, known as public speaking. This might sound scary, but public speaking was very important!

An ancient Roman calculator was known as an abacus.

Do you ever worry about getting a question wrong and looking silly? Well, thank goodness that's all that happens these days! In ancient Rome, children who could not answer a question might be beaten in front of the class. That's a terrifying thought!

Rich children who were not quite rich enough for school would have tutors. That means only one teacher would come to their house to teach all the subjects. The rest of ancient Rome's children would be taught by their parents.

I don't know who I trust less, Mum and Dad or these tutors!

Don't worry, son. I know what I'm talking about!

School didn't have so many subjects when you were poor. If you learnt anything, it might only be how to read and write. It doesn't sound too hard, but remember: your parents probably didn't go to school, either. Let's hope they know the basics!

Children started getting ready for their futures in school. Boys would learn how to be warriors. If there was no war by the time they were old enough, they would be taught how to do their father's job.

I healed all my brother's warrior injuries, but my 'job' is collecting flowers!

Girls, on the other hand, might learn some things from their mother. However, don't start wondering how you might enjoy her job. There weren't many jobs for women in ancient Rome! Girls were taught how to run a house and be a good wife.

GROWN UP
at WHAT age?

So far, it sounds like being a kid in ancient Rome was really tough. It must have been far better to be an adult. They probably had all the fun. Well, since there were no teenagers in ancient Rome, being an adult might happen sooner than you would think!

I can't wait to be them!

Some adults having easy lives.

Girls would be thought of as women at around 12 years old. They were seen as adults at a younger age than boys. That means they can do what they want sooner, right? Actually, it might mean it's time to get married.

MARRIED? AT 12?

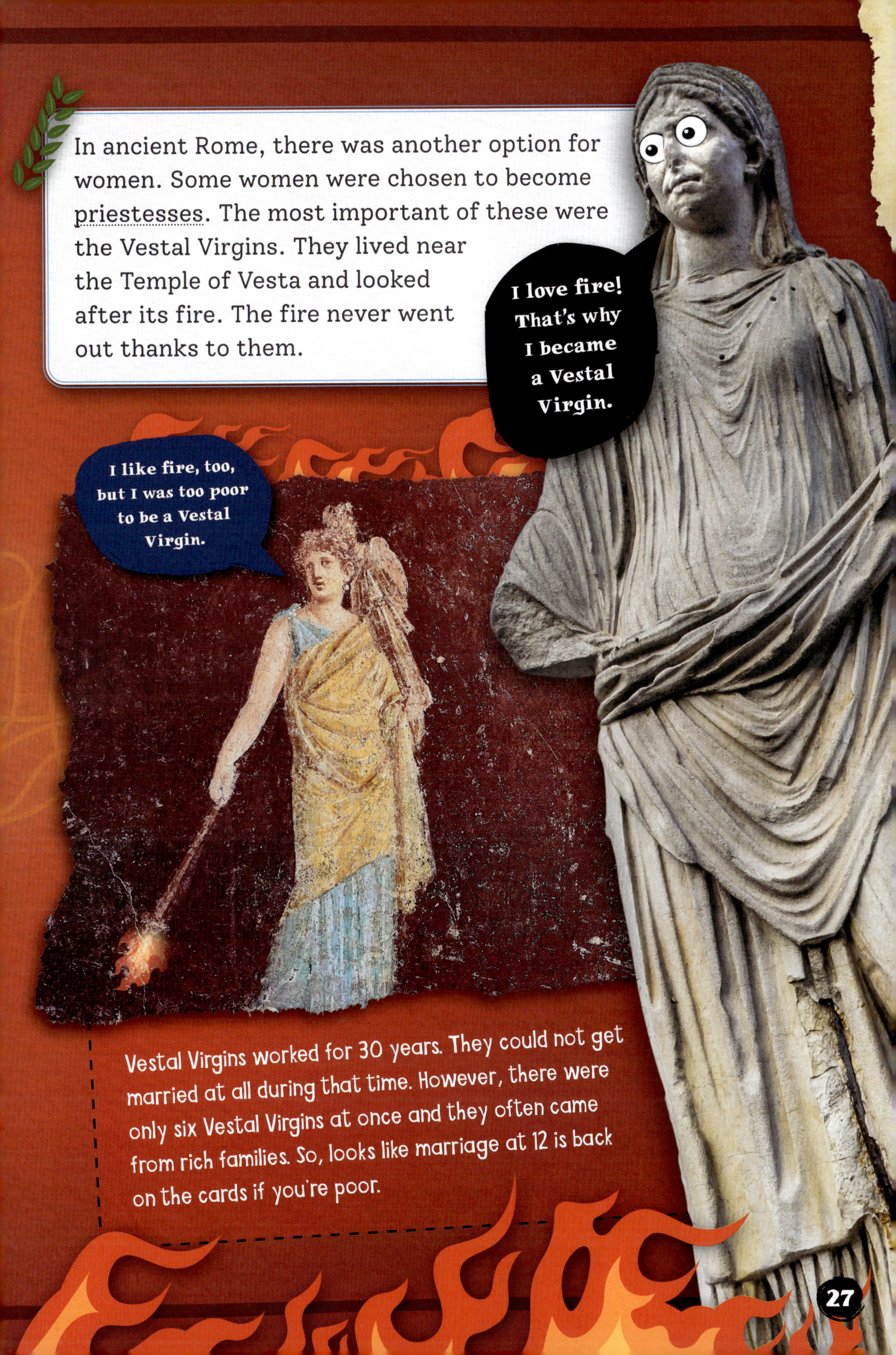

In ancient Rome, there was another option for women. Some women were chosen to become priestesses. The most important of these were the Vestal Virgins. They lived near the Temple of Vesta and looked after its fire. The fire never went out thanks to them.

I love fire! That's why I became a Vestal Virgin.

I like fire, too, but I was too poor to be a Vestal Virgin.

Vestal Virgins worked for 30 years. They could not get married at all during that time. However, there were only six Vestal Virgins at once and they often came from rich families. So, looks like marriage at 12 is back on the cards if you're poor.

As for boys, they didn't get as much of a head start at adulthood. However, they were thought of as men by around 16 or 17. Boys did not always get married straight away. That didn't mean they had it easy, either. Things could get much worse for a boy in ancient Rome.

Worse?

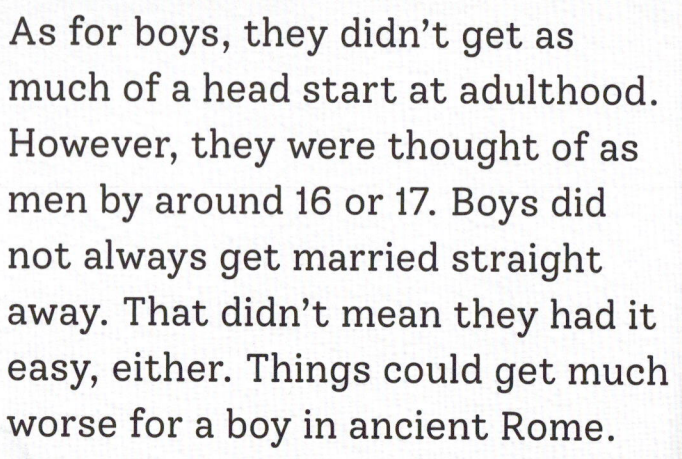

Once boys became men, they would most likely work. This could mean helping your dad bring in more money for the family. It could also mean joining the Roman army and going off to war. Of course, this only happened if there was a war on… and there were lots of wars in ancient Rome.

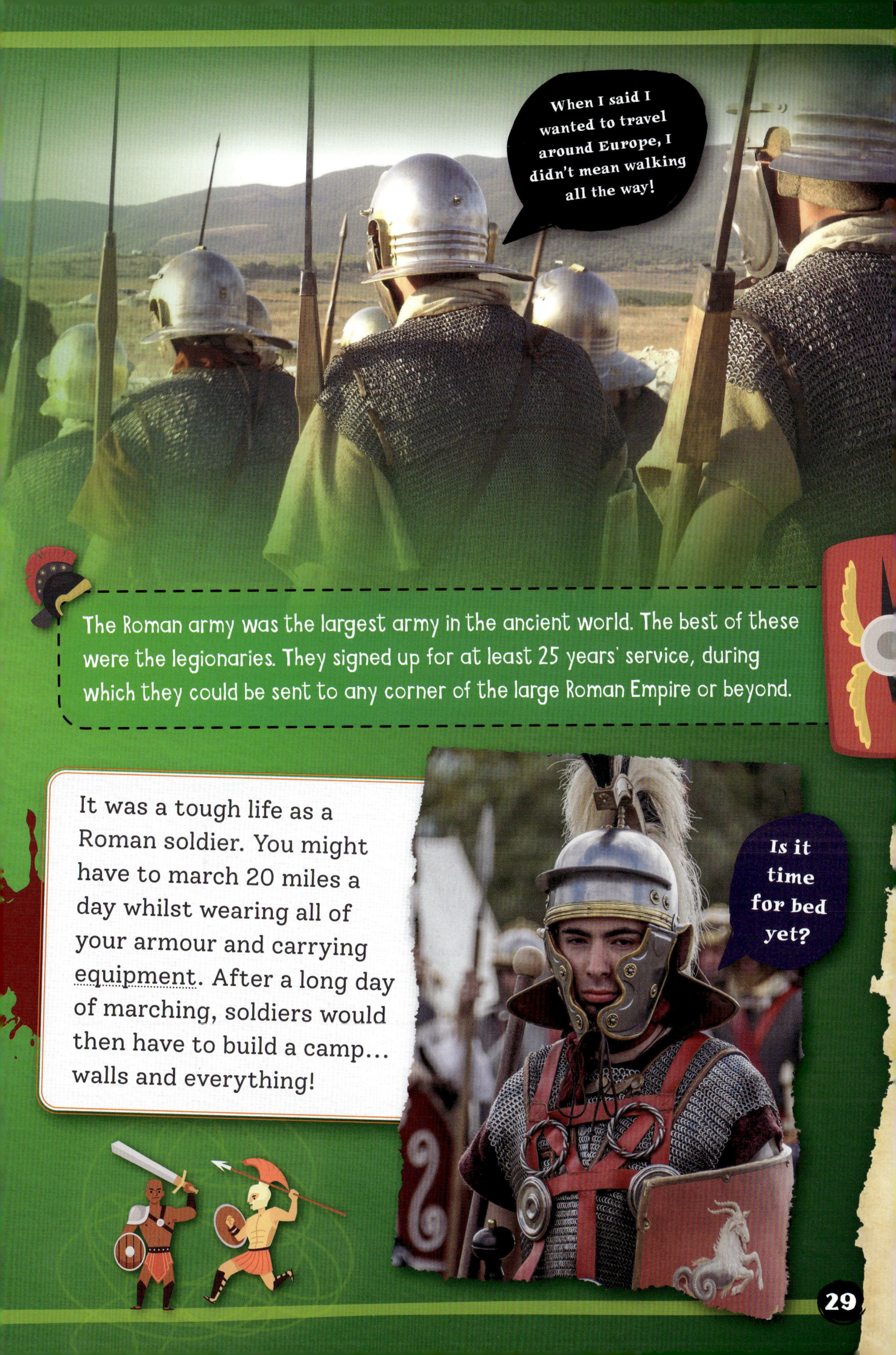

When I said I wanted to travel around Europe, I didn't mean walking all the way!

The Roman army was the largest army in the ancient world. The best of these were the legionaries. They signed up for at least 25 years' service, during which they could be sent to any corner of the large Roman Empire or beyond.

It was a tough life as a Roman soldier. You might have to march 20 miles a day whilst wearing all of your armour and carrying equipment. After a long day of marching, soldiers would then have to build a camp… walls and everything!

Is it time for bed yet?

That's TOUGH!

Do you still think being a kid today is tough? Thank goodness it's nowhere near as tough as ancient Rome! From being seen as some sort of baby alien to shared toilet time with all the family, ancient Rome was not a fun time to be a kid... and that's if you survived your childhood.

There's no need to worry, though. Relax back into the present. You don't need to share the roads with sewage and your dad won't sell you... probably. Now, let's get back to enjoying being a kid here and now.

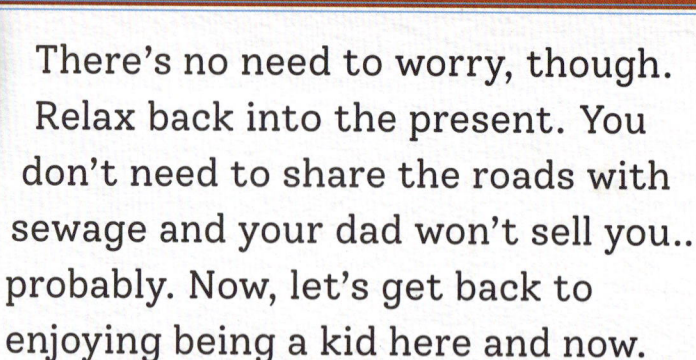

Which part of life in ancient Rome would you find the toughest?

GLOSSARY

adopt	to take a child of other parents as your own
alliances	relationships in which people agree to work together
BC	meaning 'before Christ', it is used to mark dates that occurred before the starting year of most calendars
bind	to tie or wrap something together with rope or string
ceremonies	formal acts or events
charm	an object that is believed to have magical powers
disown	to decide that someone will no longer be connected with someone else
election	the act or process of choosing someone for an important public role in a vote
electricity	something that is carried through wires to make lights and machines work
empire	a group of countries ruled by an emperor or empress
equipment	tools needed for a special purpose
herbs	a plant or a part of a plant
honour	to treat someone with respect
medicine	something that is used to treat illness or help with pain
priestesses	women who lead or perform religious ceremonies
sacrifices	acts of getting rid of something to please a god
sewage	waste from toilets
social	activities in which people spend time with each other
worshipped	showed respect to something as a god

INDEX

adoption 10

armies 28–29

babies 8, 30

board games 21

bullas 19

chores 17

doctors 9

empires 6, 29

fires 13, 17, 27

gods 16–17

knucklebones 20

marriage 26–28

maths 23

scrolls 6–7

togas 18

toilets 7, 12, 30

tunics 18–19

tutors 24

vegetables 4, 14–15

Photo Credits All images are courtesy of Shutterstock.com, unless otherwise specified. With thanks to Getty Images, Thinkstock Photo and iStockphoto.

Recurring images - YamabikaY, Tartila, TADDEUS, sumkinn, Vlada Young, Gaidamashchuk, pics five, adecvatman, Sabelskaya, dimethylorange, Andrey_Kuzmin. Cover - Gilmanshin, Marti Bug Catcher. 2-3 - S.Borisov. 4-5 - donatas1205, pisaphotography, rangizzz, s_oleg, VaLiza. 6-7 - Anna Violet, BearFotos, ben Bryant, Danilo Ascione, HappyPictures, Krakenimages.com, Oleksandr Polonskyi, pics five. YUCALORA. 8-9 - Charly Morlock, ChiccoDodiFC, Katrina Elena, Photosebia. 10-11 - Bill Perry, Charly Morlock, Massimo Todaro, Oligo22, Stefano Panzeri. 12-13 - Algol, imagoDens, Krakenimages.com, Marcos Mesa Sam Wordley, mgallar, Phant, SpicyTruffel. 14-15 - Ekaterina Zelenova, Inspiring, Kalinin Ilya, Krikkiat, magda, PaniYani, Zhuravlev Andrey. 16-17 -ASTA Concept, Azer Mess, Brenda Kean, PiercarloAbate, Romix Image, Shanvood. 18-19 - Nadzin, padu_foto, Sailko (Wikimedia Commons), Zhuravlev Andrey. 20-21 - ben Bryant, Beniho design, cigdem, David Leshem, Gilmanshin, LANO2, Xseon, Yashkin Ilya, Zhuravlev Andrey. 22-23 - mr.Ilkin, Natvas, Thesamphotography. 24-25 - GoodStudio, mountainpix, shakko (Wikimedia Commons), svetograph. 26-27 - BAZA Production, Bill Perry, BlackMac, Massimo Todaro, Prostock-studio, Yulia Serova. 28-29 - Fevziie, footageclips, FXQuadro, Gilmanshin. 30 - VaLiza.